The
SMALL and MIGHTY
Book of
Oceans

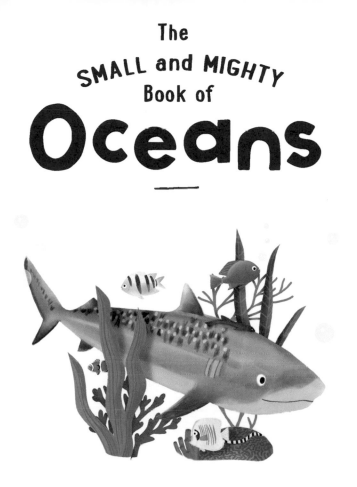

Published in 2022 by OH!.
An imprint of Welbeck Children's Limited, part of Welbeck Publishing Group.
Based in London and Sydney.

www.welbeckpublishing.com

Design and layout © Welbeck Children's Limited 2022
Text copyright © Welbeck Children's Limited 2022

Writer: Tracey Turner
Illustrator: Kirsti Davidson
Design and text by Raspberry Books Ltd
Editorial Manager: Joff Brown
Design Manager: Matt Drew
Production: Melanie Robertson

ISBN 978 1 83935 148 8

Printed in Heshan, China

10 9 8 7 6 5 4 3 2 1

FSC
www.fsc.org
MIX
Paper from
responsible sources
FSC® C020056

The
SMALL and MIGHTY
Book of
Oceans

Tracey Turner and Kirsti Davidson

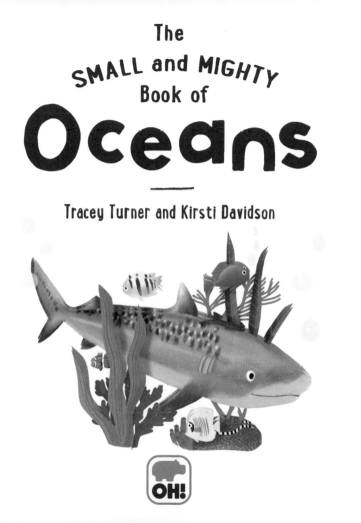

OH!

Contents

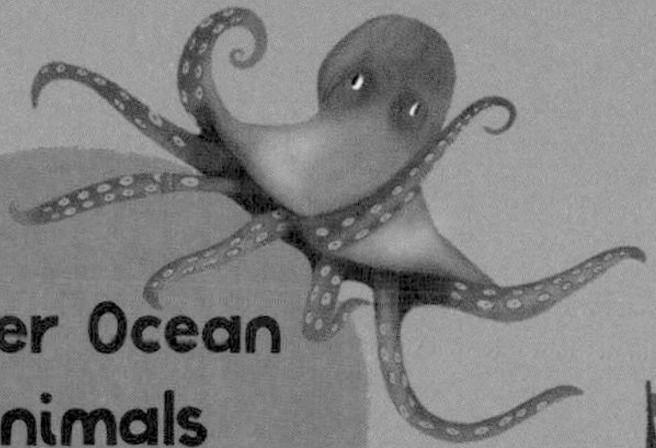

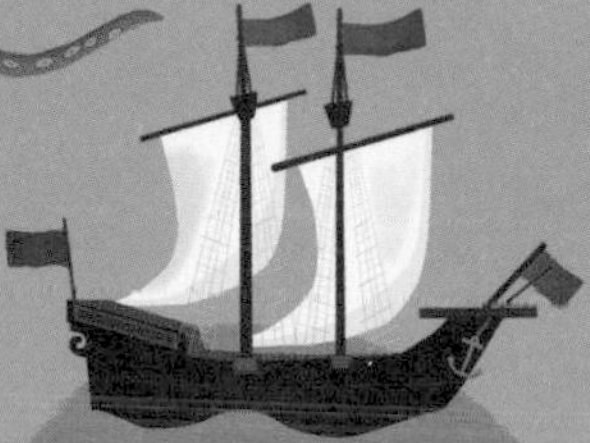

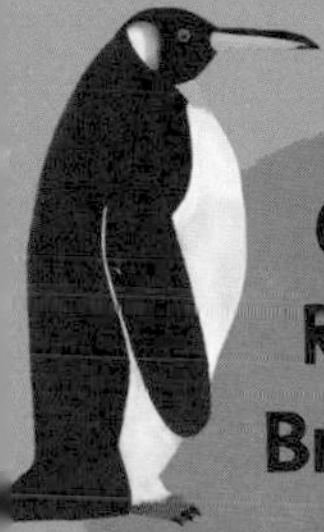

INTRODUCTION

This little book is absolutely bursting with facts about planet Earth's oceans.

Oceans cover most of the world, and under the surface lurk volcanoes, mountains, a trench almost 7 mi. deep, and the most incredible animals you'll ever meet. Discover . . .

- a creature with three brains
- fish that blow up like a balloon
- a 50,000-year-old sea voyage
- 6 ft. long tube worms
  that like a hot bath

. . . and lots more.

You'll find that the waters of the
world are full of wonders.

Ocean
Homes

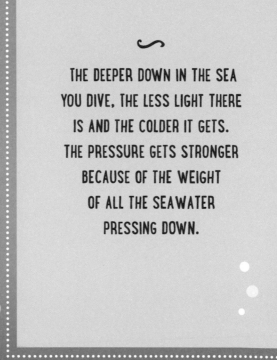

THE DEEPER DOWN IN THE SEA
YOU DIVE, THE LESS LIGHT THERE
IS AND THE COLDER IT GETS.
THE PRESSURE GETS STRONGER
BECAUSE OF THE WEIGHT
OF ALL THE SEAWATER
PRESSING DOWN.

MOST FISH AND OTHER
ANIMALS LIVE IN THE TOP
650 FT. OF THE OCEAN,
WHERE LIGHT FROM
THE SUN CAN REACH. BUT
ANIMALS LIVE FARTHER
DOWN TOO, EVEN IN THE
VERY DEEPEST PART OF
THE OCEAN, WHERE IT'S
ICY COLD AND PITCH DARK.

~

A quarter of all the different types of **OCEAN LIFE** lives in or around **CORAL REEFS**.

The world's biggest coral reef is the Great Barrier
Reef, off the coast of eastern Australia.
It measures about 1,600 mi. long and
has taken 20,000 years to form.

There are coral reefs all over the world.
Most are in warm, shallow water, but there
are also some corals in deep, cold water.

The **BLACK SWALLOWER** is a fish that can live more than 1.5 mi. deep. It has an expanding stomach so that it can eat creatures bigger than it is!

14

Most deep-sea creatures can
make light inside their bodies—
this is called **BIOLUMINESCENCE**.
The anglerfish is one of them.
It dangles a glowing light above
its mouth, luring smaller fish,
then snapping them up.

Some **OCTOPUSES** build themselves a home out of rocks. Once they're inside, some pull a rock in place behind them over the entrance, just like a front door.

HERMIT CRABS find
a shell to use as a home
to protect their soft bodies.
As they grow, they need
to find bigger
and bigger
shells to
fit them.

HYDROTHERMAL VENTS

are like underwater chimneys on the sea floor, more than 6,500 ft. deep. Superhot water full of chemicals comes billowing out of the vents, heated by molten rock inside Earth's crust.

Even these vents make homes for sea creatures, including crabs, shrimp, and giant tube worms more than 6 ft. long.

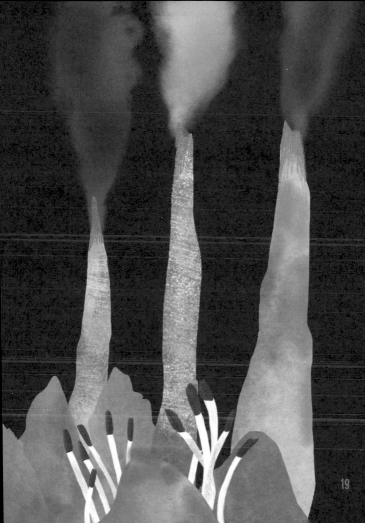

~ CLOWN FISH ~

live with sea anemones, protected within
an anemone's stinging tentacles. The
clown fish don't get hurt because of
a slimy layer on their skin. In
return, the clown fish help clean
the anemone and keep it healthy,
and chase away butterfly fish,
which nip pieces of the anemone's
tentacles if they can.

The anemone catches passing
sea creatures by shooting out
hundreds of tiny threads that
paralyze their prey. Most of
a clown fish's diet is what's
left of the anemone's food.

Very cold seas are
RICH IN PLANKTON
—tiny animals and
plants too small to see.

They are food for bigger animals.
The plants make the gas oxygen,
which all living things need. So
icy cold oceans are full of life.

Animals that live near the North Pole
include polar bears, narwhals,
and walruses.

Penguins and leopard seals
live near the South Pole.

ESTUARIES, where
rivers meet the sea,
are home to millions of **TINY CREATURES,**
including snails, worms, and shellfish,
living underneath the mud. When the tide
goes out, wading birds arrive to
eat the small animals.

MANGROVES

are trees that can live
in salty seawater along the
coast. Their long roots make
a home for animals such as
fish, shrimp, crabs, jellyfish,
alligators, and crocodiles.

The mangroves are safer
than the open sea for baby
sea creatures, including
lemon sharks.

Fishy Friends

Fish are animals that live in water and breathe through gills. There are tens of thousands of different kinds, and they can be very different from one another. Sharks are the biggest fish, eels are fish that look like snakes, and seahorses are some of the most strangely shaped fish.

Fish have lived on Earth since way before the time of the dinosaurs—beginning about **500 million** years ago!

PUFFER FISH

gulp water and then **blow up** like a **balloon**, which makes it very difficult for a predator to eat them. Many puffer fish have **spines**, so they look like spiky balloons when they blow up. They are also poisonous.

ANIMALS THAT ARE
CALLED "FISH" BUT
AREN'T ACTUALLY FISH:

1. Starfish
2. Jellyfish
3. Cuttlefish

FISH WITH UNUSUAL NAMES:

～

1. Sarcastic fringehead
2. Lumpsucker
3. Red-lipped batfish

PARROTFISH
make slime, then wrap themselves inside it before they go to sleep.

Most sand is made of tiny grains of rock and shell. But a lot of the sand on beaches near coral reefs is poop from parrotfish! Parrotfish scrape algae from rock and coral to eat, and poop out the ground-up rock and coral.

THREE FISH WITH UNUSUAL HEADS

1. SWORDFISH—
a fish named for
its swordlike bill.

2. SAW SHARK—
named for its long
nose edged with
sharp teeth, similar
to a saw.

3. WINGHEAD SHARK—
has the widest head of
all hammerhead sharks,
up to 3 ft. wide.

36

MILLIONS OF SARDINES MIGRATE ALONG THE COAST
OF SOUTH AFRICA IN SCHOOLS THAT CAN BE
4 MI. LONG, 1 MI. WIDE AND 100 FT. DEEP.

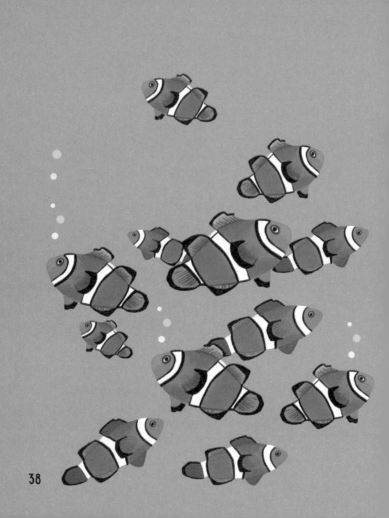

All **CLOWN FISH** are born male. Some change into females later on, when they become the leader of the clown fish group.

THE EARLIEST TYPES OF SHARKS lived around 400 million years ago—more than 150 million years before the first dinosaurs.

remora fish

REMORA FISH hang on to sharks and other big sea creatures using a **SUCKER** on top of their heads. They get a free ride—and also free meals from the bigger animal's leftovers.

RAYS

are flat fish and close relatives
of sharks. Like sharks, they use
a **special sense** that picks up
electrical signals in the water
to help them find their prey.

Electric rays can make a strong
electric current, which they use if
they feel threatened by another
animal or to **stun animals**
they want to eat.

43

≋

A SWORDFISH gets its name because of its long, thin bill, which is part of its jawbone. Swordfish slash at smaller fish with their pointy bills. The fish that are stunned or injured are easier to catch and eat.

COELACANTHS

ARE FISH THAT HAVE LIVED
ON EARTH FOR A VERY LONG
TIME. THEY WERE THOUGHT
TO HAVE DIED OUT AROUND
66 MILLION YEARS AGO,
UNTIL ONE WAS CAUGHT IN
A FISHING NET IN 1938.

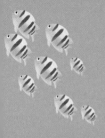

TIGER SHARKS

are not picky eaters. They usually eat **fish, sea mammals, seabirds, and turtles,** but they've been known to eat all sorts of things, including a **license plate,** car tires, and other trash.

There are
more than 47
different kinds of
SEAHORSES.
These four are named
after other animals:

1. Giraffe seahorse
2. Hedgehog seahorse
3. Tiger tail seahorse
4. Zebra seahorse

Female seahorses lay eggs, then the **MALE SEAHORSES** carry them in a special pouch until the baby seahorses hatch out of the eggs.

50

Seabirds and Mammals

~ MAMMALS ~

are warm-blooded animals
and include human beings, bears,
dolphins and many more.
Sea mammals rely on the ocean
to live—they might live in the sea
all the time, like whales, or spend
most of their time on land,
like polar bears.

There are hundreds
of different kinds of
seabirds, which also
need the sea to survive.

THERE ARE 18 DIFFERENT KINDS OF PENGUINS:

1. Adelie
2. African
3. Chinstrap
4. Emperor
5. Erect-crested
6. Fiordland
7. Galapagos
8. Gentoo
9. Humboldt
10. King
11. Little blue
12. Macaroni
13. Magellanic
14. Northern rockhopper
15. Royal
16. Southern rockhopper
17. Snares
18. Yellow-eyed

Penguins live in the Southern Hemisphere—
the southern half of the world—except
for one kind, the Galapagos penguin,
which is sometimes seen in the
Northern Hemisphere.

55

WHALES and DOLPHINS

spend all their lives in the sea.
But because they are mammals,
they need to come up to the
surface to **BREATHE AIR**.

Instead of relying on sight alone, some whales and dolphins make sounds that **BOUNCE OFF OBJECTS** in the sea around them, then bounce back to the animals' ears.

This gives them an excellent "SOUND PICTURE" of their surroundings. This clever trick is called "ECHOLOCATION."

POLAR BEARS ARE MARINE
MAMMALS AND THE WORLD'S
BIGGEST MEAT EATERS ON LAND.
THEY ARE VERY GOOD SWIMMERS
AND HAVE BEEN SPOTTED
SWIMMING 60 MI. AWAY
FROM LAND.

UNDERNEATH ITS FUR,
A POLAR BEAR'S SKIN
IS BLACK. THE HAIRS
ARE SEE-THROUGH AND
HOLLOW. THEY APPEAR
WHITE BECAUSE LIGHT
BOUNCES AROUND INSIDE
THE HOLLOW HAIRS AND
THIS LOOKS WHITE TO
OUR EYES.

～ The ～
WANDERING ALBATROSS

spends almost all its time flying over the sea. It has the longest wingspan of any bird—more than 10 ft. It uses its enormous wings to cruise along on currents of air, traveling many thousands of miles.

DOLPHINS are famous for acrobatic displays, and the spinner dolphin is the most spectacular of all—it leaps out of the water and spins around in midair.

There are 36 kinds of
dolphins that live in the sea—
ORCAS are the BIGGEST.

There are also five kinds
of river dolphins, two of which
are only found in the Amazon.

Bottlenose dolphins can keep
one half of their brain awake
while the other half sleeps
so that they can rest but be
on the alert for danger
at the same time.

~ WALRUSES ~
can weigh up to
1.5 TONS.

Even a newborn baby walrus weighs more than an average adult human.

Both male and female walruses have enormous tusks that can measure 3 ft. long. They use them like sticks to haul themselves out of the water and onto the land, and also to smash breathing holes in sea ice.

HUMPBACK WHALES

spend the summer in cold seas
near the Antarctic, then travel
around 3,000 mi. to warmer
waters in the Pacific Ocean
for the winter.

NARWHALS

are whales with a single long, **spiral tusk.** The tusk can measure **10 ft.** long—about the same as three seven-year-old children standing on one another's shoulders. Only male narwhals have the long tusk—females either don't have one at all or just have a short one.

THERE ARE SEVEN KINDS OF SEA TURTLES IN THE WORLD:

1. Leatherback
2. Loggerhead
3. Green
4. Hawksbill
5. Flatback
6. Olive Ridley
7. Kemp's Ridley

LEATHERBACK TURTLES are the largest kind and weigh up to 2,000 lb. *Archelon* was a prehistoric sea turtle that weighed more than 2 tons! It died out sometime between 83 million and 65 million years ago.

Sea turtles often eat jellyfish. Sadly, the turtles sometimes mistake plastic bags for jellyfish, which can harm the animals if they eat them.

Male
BLUE-FOOTED BOOBIES

have bright blue webbed feet. They strut around showing off their feet to female blue-footed boobies. The bluer their feet, the more attractive the female boobies think they are.

There are **SIX** different kinds of boobies. Red-footed boobies are the smallest kind, and many of them have blue beaks that contrast with their red feet.

PUFFINS

can hold several fish in their mouths at once because their rough tongues and **spiny mouths** give them a firm grip. This means they can bring back plenty of food in one trip to give to their chicks.

Puffins are excellent swimmers. They can dive down to 200 ft. deep in search of their fishy prey.

Puffins have bright orange beaks and feet only in the spring and summer—the rest of the year they're much duller, and their beaks are smaller because they shed the outer layer.

～ SEALS ～
and SEA LIONS

are ocean mammals called "pinnipeds."
The difference between them is that sea lions
can walk along on land on their big flippers,
while seals' flippers are only useful
for swimming—on land they shuffle
along on their stomachs.

Sea lions also have ear flaps that you can
see, but you can't see a seal's ears.

Sea lions are noisy animals. They make a loud barking noise, while seals tend to be much quieter.

Walruses are pinnipeds too.

You can tell a

BLUE WHALE'S

age by its earwax! During the course of the whale's life, new layers of earwax form in its ears. Scientists can figure out the age of the animal by looking at the wax.

Most blue whales live to about **80 or 90 years old**, but the oldest one found so far was about **110**, according to its earwax.

Other Ocean Animals

The SEA takes up more of EARTH'S SURFACE than the land

and is home to a wide variety of different creatures. As well as all the fish, seabirds, and mammals that live in the ocean, there are reptiles (such as turtles), mollusks (including octopuses and squid) and many more weird and wonderful animals.

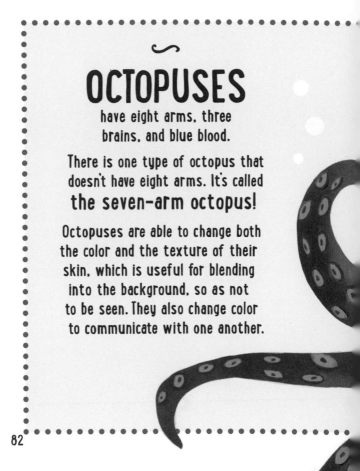

OCTOPUSES

have eight arms, three brains, and blue blood.

There is one type of octopus that doesn't have eight arms. It's called **the seven-arm octopus!**

Octopuses are able to change both the color and the texture of their skin, which is useful for blending into the background, so as not to be seen. They also change color to communicate with one another.

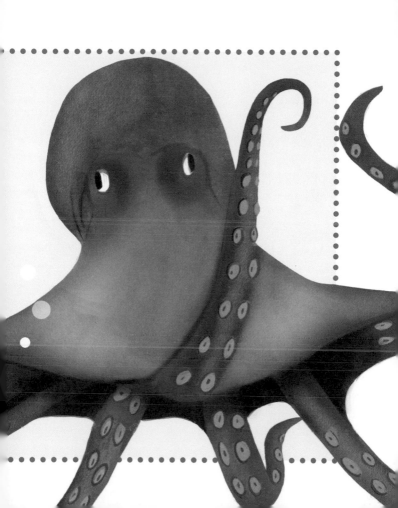

SQUID, CUTTLEFISH, OYSTERS, SCALLOPS, AND OCTOPUSES are all types of marine **MOLLUSKS**.

Most mollusks live in the sea, but there are mollusks on land too, including snails and slugs (and there are also sea snails and sea slugs).

Unlike land slugs, some sea slugs are **VERY BRIGHTLY COLORED**. The colors warn away animals that might want to eat them.

SEA SNAKES are some of the most venomous snakes in the world. They aren't usually dangerous to people, because they are shy creatures and have short fangs that deliver only a small amount of venom.

STARFISH

aren't fish. They belong to a group of animals called echinoderms, which also includes sea urchins. There are around 1,600 different kinds of starfish.

Most starfish have five arms surrounding a disk-shaped body in the middle. But there are also starfish with 10, 20, 40, and even 50 arms.

If starfish lose or damage an arm, they can regrow it! Sometimes starfish shed an arm if they're attacked, allowing them to get away, ready to grow a new arm.

90

Jellyfish don't have eyes or a brain.

Their bag-like bodies trail long, stinging tentacles, which they use to paralyze prey before eating it.

Some jellyfish **glow in the dark.**

STARFISH

eat other animals, including **shellfish**, **sea snails**, and **worms**. Some starfish have an unusual way of eating animals like mussels and scallops. The starfish pushes its stomach out of its mouth, engulfing the soft parts of the animal it's about to eat.

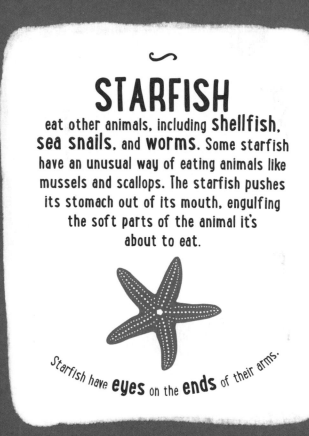

Starfish have **eyes** on the **ends** of their arms.

SOME STARFISH WITH INTERESTING NAMES:

~

1. Chocolate chip sea star
2. Sunflower star
3. Arctic cookie star
4. Pincushion star
5. Crown-of-thorns starfish

Coral reefs are made up of millions of individual coral polyps, which are tiny animals related to jellyfish and sea anemones. Hard corals build a skeleton outside their bodies, which is how coral reefs are formed. These reefs are found in warm, shallow water.

Soft corals are soft and flexible, and look
like plants (but they're animals too).
They don't have a stony skeleton
like hard corals. They are found in warm,
shallow water and in deep, cold water.

~ SEA SNAKES ~

breathe air, like we do,
so they have to come to the surface
of the ocean for air. But some sea snakes
can also take in oxygen from the water
through their skin straight into
their blood, which is the same as
what happens in a fish's gills.

We don't know much about

GIANT
SQUID

because they live deep in the ocean and are good at hiding from people who want to study them. One of the biggest ever discovered was almost 60 ft. long.

People and the Sea

WE COULDN'T LIVE WITHOUT
THE OCEAN.

People have always relied on it for food and transportation. Long ago, people set sail to EXPLORE NEW LANDS by sea.

The ocean is HUGE, and most of it is still waiting to be explored. So far, we've only made maps of about one-fifth of the sea floor and only explored a tiny amount of the entire ocean.

101

The sea can be **DANGEROUS**, especially long ago when it was more difficult for sailors to find their way and ships weren't as safe as they are today. Sailors told stories about terrifying **SEA MONSTERS**.

One of them was the **KRAKEN**, a giant squid, octopus, or sometimes a crab. It was more than **A MILE** long, and stories said it could pick up sailing ships and hurl them into the air.

The ancient Greeks told stories about the sea monsters **SCYLLA** and **CHARYBDIS**. Scylla was a six-headed, snake-like monster. Charybdis sucked up sea water and made a dangerous whirlpool with it, sinking ships. Avoiding one monster meant sailing close to the other one.

Many people like eating fish.
But one of the strangest
and most expensive
fish on the menu is a type of

PUFFER FISH,

known as fugu.

Chefs need to train for years
before they can prepare fugu,
because it's so poisonous
that it can kill people if
they eat the wrong part.

~

SHARK ATTACKS ARE VERY RARE.
BUT THESE ARE THE THREE KINDS
OF SHARKS RESPONSIBLE FOR THE
MOST ATTACKS ON PEOPLE:

~

1. **Great white sharks**
   (which can measure 23 ft. long)

2. **Bull sharks**
   (around 8 ft. long)

3. **Tiger sharks**
   (mostly around 10 ft. long).

There are many different kinds of sharks —more than 400—and most are not dangerous to humans.

Sharks are in **more danger** from us than we are from them—people kill 100 million sharks and rays every year!

~ WALRUSES ALMOST DIED OUT ~ because people used to hunt them

for their meat, tusks, and skin in the 1600s to 1800s. Today, walrus hunting is allowed only for certain groups of people who depend on them to live. These people have to make sure they don't hunt so many walruses that they put them in danger of dying out.

~ STONEFISH ~

can be very dangerous to people.
They look stony like the seabed and are
hard to see against the ocean floor.
When they feel threatened, they
raise long spines on their back
that INJECT VENOM, which is
very painful and has been
known to kill people.

A bite from a
BLUE-RINGED OCTOPUS
is enough to kill an adult human. These small but deadly creatures —only the size of a golf ball— are some of the most venomous animals in the world.

TODAY'S OCEAN EXPLORERS SEND ROBOTS TO MAP THE SEABED AND TAKE PHOTOGRAPHS. IN THE PAST, PEOPLE SET SAIL INTO UNCHARTED TERRITORY TO EXPLORE THE WORLD.

1. Some of the FIRST EXPLORERS in the world were the people who sailed on rafts to the continent of Australia, around 50,000 years ago. They (probably) had to cross around 55 mi. of open sea.

2. Viking explorer LEIF ERIKSON sailed from Iceland to what's now Canada around the year 1000.

3. In 1492, CHRISTOPHER COLUMBUS made a famous sea voyage from Europe across the Atlantic Ocean (but he never landed on the American mainland).

4. The first people to sail all the way around the world were some of FERDINAND MAGELLAN's crew in the 1500s.

5. In the 1700s, Captain JAMES COOK made the first accurate map of the Pacific Ocean.

Our oceans are in danger because of human beings.

The world is getting warmer, because of people using fuels such as oil, coal, and natural gas, which add the gas carbon dioxide to Earth's atmosphere.

In the ocean, carbon dioxide threatens many kinds of sea animals. It can damage coral reefs and make it difficult for sea creatures to make shells.

We need to stop putting more carbon dioxide into the atmosphere and into the ocean. Organizations such as Greenpeace, the World Wildlife Fund, Oceana, and the Coral Reef Alliance are working hard to protect our oceans.

Ocean Record Breakers

Most of
the surface of
Earth is water,
and most of that
water is oceans. It's
the biggest animal
habitat on Earth.

THE PACIFIC OCEAN IS THE
BIGGEST OF THE WORLD'S
OCEANS—IN FACT, IT COVERS
ABOUT A THIRD OF THE SURFACE
OF EARTH. IT STRETCHES
FROM THE SOUTHERN OCEAN,
AROUND ANTARCTICA IN THE
SOUTHERNMOST PART OF THE
WORLD, TO THE ARCTIC IN THE FAR
NORTH. IT'S MORE THAN TWICE
THE SIZE OF THE NEXT-BIGGEST
OCEAN, THE ATLANTIC.

The **BIGGEST ANIMAL** that's ever lived on planet Earth is the

BLUE WHALE.

It's bigger than any dinosaur.

A blue whale can be **105 ft.** long and weigh **200 tons.** Even a newborn baby blue whale weighs more than a hippo. These huge creatures live on tiny things—they scoop up and eat shrimp-like creatures called krill.

A blue whale's heart weighs about the same as a full-grown bottlenose dolphin.

The
BIGGEST
FISH

in the world is the whale shark, which can measure more than 40 ft. long and weigh around 15 tons.

One of the smallest fish ever discovered is less than half an inch long. It only has a Latin name—*Paedocypris progenetica*.

The **GREENLAND SHARK** is the world's **LONGEST-LIVING FISH,** and also the world's **LONGEST-LIVING ANIMAL WITH A BACKBONE.** The oldest one ever discovered is a female shark thought to be around 400 years old—she was born not long after William Shakespeare wrote *Hamlet* and the telescope was invented.

Greenland sharks grow
very slowly and aren't
mature adults
until they're about
150 years old!

⁓The⁓
LONGEST
MOUNTAIN RANGE

in the world is under the sea.
The Mid-Ocean Ridge stretches all the
way around the world in zigzags,
about 40,400 mi. long. On land, the
longest mountain range is the Andes,
which is about 4,350 mi. long.

To make it even more exciting,
the **Mid-Ocean Ridge is a series
of volcanoes, where most of the
world's volcanic eruptions happen.**
As a result, it's changing all the time.
New rock is formed when the volcanoes
erupt and becomes part of Earth's crust.

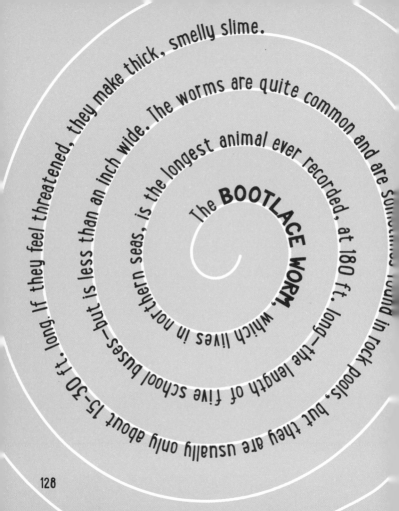

The **BOOTLACE WORM**, which lives in northern seas, is the longest animal ever recorded, at 180 ft. long—the length of five school buses—but is less than an inch wide. The worms are quite common and are sometimes found in rock pools, but they are usually only about 15–30 ft. long. If they feel threatened, they make thick, smelly slime.

128

The
COLOSSAL
SQUID

has the largest eyes of any animal in the world—they measure about 10 in. across, the size of a dinner plate.

The deepest part of the ocean is Challenger Deep,

in the Mariana Trench in the Pacific Ocean. It's almost 7 mi. deep. If you could stand Mount Everest with its base at the bottom of Challenger Deep, there would still be more than a mile of water between Mount Everest's summit and the surface of the ocean.

Even at the very deepest part of
Challenger Deep there are living
things, including bacteria and
shrimp-like creatures.

IT'S DIFFICULT TO MEASURE HOW
FAST A FISH CAN SWIM...

...one of the fastest is the BLACK MARLIN, which has been recorded speeding through the water in short bursts of 80 mph—that's almost as fast as a cheetah can run on land.

THE BIGGEST TYPE
OF JELLYFISH IS THE
LION'S MANE JELLYFISH.
IT CAN MEASURE MORE THAN
6.5 FT. ACROSS, AND ITS
STINGING TENTACLES CAN
BE OVER 100 FT. LONG.

THE SPERM WHALE
HAS THE LARGEST BRAIN
OF ANY ANIMAL IN THE
WORLD. IT'S ALSO THE
LARGEST TOOTHED WHALE,
MEASURING UP TO
65 FT. LONG.

~

The biggest living structure
on Earth is the
GREAT BARRIER REEF,
which measures
around 1,400 mi. long.

The OCEANIC MANTA RAY

is the world's **biggest ray**—it can measure **23 ft.** across and weigh 2 tons. The smallest type of ray, the shortnose electric ray, measures only about 4 in. across and weighs 14 oz. The manta ray is 2,500 times bigger!

As far as we know, the largest fish that ever lived was the megalodon, a type of shark that could reach 50 ft. long. It died out around 2.6 million years ago.

The

WORLD'S BIGGEST

sea lions are

STELLER SEA LIONS,

which can weigh more than a ton.

They eat fish, squid,
and octopuses and are found
in the northern
Pacific Ocean.

∽ Southern ∽
ELEPHANT SEALS

are the biggest kind of seals and are much larger than Steller sea lions. The largest males can **weigh 4 tons**—up to four times as much as female elephant seals or Steller sea lions, and more than the **biggest** hippopotamus.

EMPEROR PENGUINS

are the biggest penguins in the world, up to 4 ft. tall and 100 lb. in weight.

Emperor penguins are also the deepest-diving birds. The deepest ever recorded was 1,850 ft. below the surface of the sea.

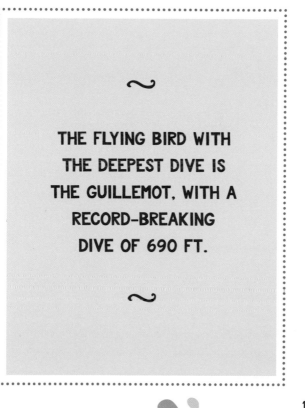

THE FLYING BIRD WITH
THE DEEPEST DIVE IS
THE GUILLEMOT, WITH A
RECORD-BREAKING
DIVE OF 690 FT.